A Talk on Rhyme

# A Talk on Rhyme

*and*

# A Bibliography on Rhyme and Related Issues

*by*

David Brazil

The Yellow Papers 4 . Amsterdam, 2021

*Note*: The timestamps in the margins of this text are keyed to a recording of the original talk, which as of Sept. 2021 is available at berlspoetry.com/recordings/2014/10/20/leslie-flint-presents-david-brazil-introduced-by-ian-dreiblatt/.

# A Talk on Rhyme

[*As an overture to the talk, I sang "Take Me to the River," following Al Green's arrangement.*]

Thank you so much, everybody. Thank you very much. I'm really happy to be here. Thank you, Ian, for that terrific and apposite introduction. Thanks to the folks at Berl's for this opportunity. And thanks also in absentia to Jamie Townsend, who invited me to do this but couldn't be here. But I love him and miss him and think of him with some frequency.

So I was really happy to be invited to Leslie Flint, but it's a little in some ways daunting because being a single reader sort of puts you on the spot and it's an invitation to move around with a lot of space, both in terms of the temporality, but also in terms of the form.

And because it's an opportunity to do anything you want, you kind of have to think about like, gosh, what do I actually want to do outside of the given generic form of the two-reader reading or the three-reader reading or whatever, you know, you all know these genres. So I thought what I'd actually like to do most is to think and talk about things that have been preoccupying me that I don't really have answers to and that you all might be able to help me think about.

And I kind of wanted to engage in what I think of as a piece of kind of public thinking around this stuff, illustrated with examples from my recent work and sort of historical divagations and maybe with some time to talk with folks about, you know, some feedback on some of this stuff.

And what I really wanted to talk about, and it's really good to be doing this in Berl's Poetry Shop, is rhyme; that's actually what I've been really preoccupied with lately. So my talk and presentation is going to be about rhyme. And I'll open with one thing which not only rhymes but is actually a sonnet, because I've been writing sonnets lately, and then I go from there. But this is something that I wrote this week for y'all. So it's for you. Take it if you want.

6:36
> Rime is the body of my resurrection
> made apostolic in portals from here
> so that the after will yield a correction
> to each mortal garment and each earthly fear
>
> When time is the instrument grace is the measure
> for each passing lineament mercy cant hold
> and when o my love shall we have the leisure
> to see how each would that we are might unfold.
>
> We bring them forth out of our sovereign appointments
> with hours that shine in the mornings like stars
> and then like the oil of priestly anointments
> point up just where in the circuit we are.
>
> I answer blessings outside of a prose,
> for we are not on the earth as you suppose.

So that's one of the sonnets I've been writing lately, and I wanted to use that as the overture and then frame what I want to talk about with two different text extracts. And I didn't have the time to prepare handouts—I would have loved to just made a little zine for you all you could take home or put on the wall with

## on Rhyme

some of these extracts that I had in mind. But hearing me say them—and I'd be happy to repeat them—will have to do.

The first one is a bit that comes from a book by Giorgio Agamben I have been turning over in my mind for years. It's his book on Paul and the letter to the Romans that's called *The Time that Remains*—came out in like '99. It's a terrific book, not just about Paul, but about religion in general and about messianic time, which is his theme. And he connects Paul with Walter Benjamin and kind of creates a historical rhyme between Paul's text to the Romans and Benjamin's "Theses on the Philosophy of History" with which many of you are familiar.

And that's a thing to say about rhyme at the outset—with rhyme, I do mean end-rhyme, what we think of when we think of rhyme, but also rhyme as kind of a metonymy for form as such, right? Any kind of closed form or formal features that govern a poem, the structural principles of poetry. And then on top of those two things—that it's rhyme as such, and that it's a metonymy for structure—that also there is a larger kind of idea of what rhyme could mean. There's formal rhymes across the arts and there's all kinds of rhymes that you could call ontological rhymes or something like that that are much bigger sort of historical rhymes in how we live. You know, rhymes between cities, rhymes between periods as Ian kind of was adducing and which is very relevant to the late epoch of American capital, where Egypt seems like a very helpful analogue. I live across the San Francisco Bay from the Transamerica Pyramid, which is there satanically looking at me every morning.

# 8 *A Talk*

So rhyme very broadly. Agamben sort of puts these figures who normally are thought of as totally separate and rhymes them. And so in his book, he has this aside where he does a reading of a sestina, one of the first sestinas, by Arnaut Daniel, a troubadour poet who wrote in Provençal. And he reads the sestina, and he reads the temporality of the sestina, according to its retrograde progression of the rhymes, and has this interesting argument about what that metaphorizes.

And at the end his discussion he has this passage that I really have been thinking about, and I've read this book many times and I've been thinking about this passage for just years, so I wanted to read it as one half of a diptych to frame the stuff I'm going to talk about. So this is Agamben: "I would like to end our exegesis of messianic time with the following hypothesis. Rhyme, understood in the broad sense of the term as the articulation of a difference between semiotic series and semantic series, is the messianic heritage that Paul leaves to modern poetry,"—rhyme is the messianic heritage Paul (Saint Paul!) leaves to contemporary poetry—"and the history and fate of rhyme coincide in poetry with the history and fate of the messianic announcement."

So, you know, that's a pretty heavy thing to bite off. And then he has a little bit that I didn't copy out from the same passage about Hölderlin. And Agamben says that we can date a moment in the history of the West to Hölderlin's thematic concern with the retreat of the gods, the withdrawal of the gods from the human world, and potentially even with the withdrawal of Christ, the last God for Hölderlin, and the ruin of Hölderlin's prosodic orientation, which had been using classical meters and sort of arrived at the late, you know, works in free rhythm that nobody really knows how to characterize, that people have studied and have often been anticipated as sort of harbingers of modern poetics, which were so important for Celan and all kinds of people who work with fragmentation.

So anyway, at the end of this little discussion of Hölderlin, Agamben says: "the absence of the gods is one with the disappearance of closed metrical form; atheology immediately becomes a-prosody," right? So, again, this kind of crazy, sort of Heideggerian claim about the intimacy of poetry with being as such, which is on the one hand obviously sort of nuts, but on the other hand, maybe it's true?

And if you're a poet, I think you're definitely interested. And I have been provoked by it for a long time.

And then the other thing I wanted to read, which I think kind of rhymes with that on the subject, is a little passage, which again, has been bugging me for years. And it comes from Jack Spicer's "Textbook of Poetry," which is, of course, such a fertile text, also totally concerned with Christ, among other things.

So this is Section 17 of Spicer's "Textbook of Poetry." And he says:

> — A human love object is untrue.
> Screw you.
>
> — A divine love object is unfair
> Define the air
> It walks in.

The old human argument goes on with the rhymes to show that it still goes on. A stiffening in time as puns are a stiffening in meaning.

12:27

> The old human argument that goes ahead with our clothes off or our clothes on. Even then, when we are talking of ghosts.
>
> — A human love object is untrue.
>   Screw you.
>
> — A divine love object is unfair
>   Define the air
>   It walks in.
>
> Imagine this as lyric poetry.

And I think that it's just such a beautiful moment where he says, *Imagine this as lyric poetry*. What I just wrote—this sort of obvious doggerel, this will to doggerel, which always reminds me of like the dumbest Velvet Underground lyrics or the dumbest Pixies lyrics or whatever your version of that is, or the very will to dumbness in the rhyme is somehow part of the aesthetic effect. I've always been super intrigued by that.

But I guess that, you know, in a way that's what we get out of rhyme at this point? What I get from the Agamben thing is that rhyme seems inoperative, right? Like rhyme just doesn't work. It's not aesthetically plausible. And I think this is the lived experience of rhyme by people receiving poetry in the twentieth and the twenty-first century. And the only way that it becomes plausible is as intentional kitsch, as ironic, or maybe in light verse, that is to say, in the form of poetry. In music, it still seems to work totally fine— and in fact, to have like an authentic charge of pathos potentially. And for me, that's a really open question— why is it the case that people can really like, you know, Dylan or Joni Mitchell or Jay-Z or whoever you think of when you think of a really amazing rhymer in music?

## on Rhyme

Is it the melody that's carrying it? Is it the voice that's carrying it? Whereas who is the last poet who authentically makes rhyme work in English, like as a real primary thing? Is it, like, Yeats? It's probably Yeats, or if it's not Yeats, it's somebody from that period. People work in rhyme, but they don't like build their career and their thought on rhyme. So I've just been really interested in that.

Like, why is it inoperative? Why does it suddenly seem to become inoperative? And this is connected to the larger question of why rhyme is a metonymy for formal principles as such? Why is there a passage from the plausibility of a certain structural principle in verse, whether it's rhyme, closed form, metrical considerations? Why does that wane? Why does it disappear? And in some ways like this, I mean, maybe it's just a mystery and a kind of head-scratcher question about the larger character of historical change.

That's part of the larger mystery. And I guess rhyme then becomes a symptom for me, of this mystery. So to read a little more of my own work, having put some sort of more prosy verbiage in the air, I wanted to read this thing that I wrote. And I'm very happy to see David Larsen joined us. And it's good timing because I did a translation from a Syriac poem.

So, you know, I'm always happy to let David hear that—which appeared in this magazine called *The Emerald Tablet*.

[Audience member: *Who's it by?*]
It's anonymous. I'll talk about it maybe after I read it. But now I've got to find it in this crazy book. Here we go. OK, um, so yeah, this is like a ballad basically, and it's called "The Hymn of the Twin in Prison":

## A Talk

16:25
I was a prince
at home with dad
that's the best time
I ever had

Born in the east
dad sent me west
and so I went
at his behest

And as I travelled
thru this nation
my whole armor
was vocation

But lost my robe
which wove from love
had been my coat
from kin above

And what ought I
do in this world?
*American,
bring back the pearl*

*it's hid out west
by snakes that dream
your precious robe
wove without seam*

*and with your twin
you'll be their heir*
so I went west
like on a dare

The road was hard
I young to tread
I saw the towns
I met the dead

## on Rhyme

Went past Babel
Babel the great
went farther west
to meet my fate

to seek the snake
who rules this world
to find his cave
and seize his pearl

I blended in
became opaque
to get the pearl
and dodge the snake

and lost, alone,
in grief I sank
so deep in woe
I drank and drank

and this prince turned
slave to their king
forgot the pearl
I'd meant to bring

Western burdens
had made me sleep
my parents saw
it made them weep

and send a word
from out their gates
to eastern earls
and magistrates

they wove a plan
that I be healed
this letter wrote,
by each one sealed:

# A Talk

*From your dad king*
*and mom also*
*and your twin too*
*to you : Hello!*

*Time that you wake*
*son we must save*
*recall, you're prince,*
*and see, you're slave*

*Recall the pearl*
*for which you went*
*recall the robe*
*for which you're meant*

*Which you will wear*
*at princes' gate*
*When twin and you*
*we'll coronate*

This letter sealed
by the king's hand
so Babel's sons
can't understand

This letter came
in a dove's form
stood next to me
that I be warned

It shook its plumes
and I awoke
and kissed the bird
and that bird spoke

I was equal
to this letter
prince I am and
I want better

## on Rhyme

And for the pearl
I'd meant to take
I sang a charm
to lull the snake

I lulled the snake
by my dad's name
and by my mom's
great eastern fame

I seized the pearl
and hit the road
abandoning
my heavy load

and went straight east
from whence comes dawn
the letter saved
and drew me on

With voice it woke
with light it led
with guidance it
drew me ahead

the letter led
past Babel town
where cash goes up
and men go down

my parents sent
from divine lands
most gracious knights
who in their hands

had bore my robe
they tended me
patient as stones
by shores of sea

# A Talk

this robe I'd let
from my mind pass
now seemed to me
just like a glass

in which my self
saw self face it
we two in kind
but like one fit

just as the knights
from lands divine
were two and one
by the king's sign

engraved who'd sent
the robe to me
my raiment brought
blinding to see

with gold and ruby
jet and pearl
and gems hewn in
the other world

and diamonds sealed it
and not seams
its threads made from
celestial beams

and sapphire was
that garment's kind
in it I read
the stir of mind

starting to speak
its holy word
I knew its tones
this speech I heard

## on Rhyme 17

*That I am which*
*your father made*
*and through his works*
*I'll never fade*

And as it gave
out its command
from those knights it
came to my hand

And in my love
I came to meet
that garment which
made love complete

And therefore clothed
as in old days
I journeyed to
the gate of praise

I bowed my head
to majesty
by whose sweet will
anamnesty

At princes' gate
I met the earls
I was received
I brought the pearl

And with one voice
they told me bring
the sacred pearl
before the king

So that's "The Hymn of the Twin in Prison"—it's
a translation of a Syriac poem that is found in the
apocryphal Acts of Thomas, which is a text about the
apostle Thomas going to the east and to Syria and to

India. Eventually he's the apostle for the Indians, part of the elaborate corpus of apocryphal Christian works. But that poem is sort of spatchcocked into a prose section. It's way older. Nobody really knows. So that's the answer to the question "Who wrote it?"—it's attributed to Thomas, I guess, but it is usually understood to be a sort of Gnostic poem.

And that's a problem that's been bugging me for many years in different translated versions that I've read of this text of the Pearl (that's how it's known—it doesn't have a name—it's usually called the Pearl, the Hymn of the Pearl, or something like that). So at a certain point, I just felt like I had to do it, I had to get it out of my system and it wanted to be rhymed. And I was like, I guess I just have to do this.

And I guess I just have to go to, like, a certain willingness to be dumb and to just do rhymes, including, like, obvious rhymes, which is also part of, you know, one reason to open with the song ["Take Me to the River"] is that I like to open with songs in general. But that song sounds a lot of the themes that concern me in this talk. You know, one of them is just the ballad tradition and musical traditions in general, both sort of secular ballad traditions as well as religious hymn traditions, and just the role of music in the poetry of my generation of poets, which is really strongly present in different ways in a lot of people's work. So part of the concern with music is the concern with traditional music, like the Harry Smith Anthology and stuff like that, where you have like—there are some dumb rhymes in there man, but, you know, the melody carries it, maybe the voice carries it, I don't know, maybe it's not carried, maybe it's just bad. Maybe what

## on Rhyme

I just read was bad, I don't know. That's up to everybody, you know, different aesthetic judgments, which is one of the larger problems that I'm always concerned with, you know, the problem of living with an apparent aporia of a standard of aesthetic judgment that we're all kind of living under, you know, the sort of post-Kantian situation—like, how do we come up with a canon of judgment in order not just to judge artworks, but in order to judge and make our own artworks, as practicing artists, like what's the basis?

So different things that I've made have been in response to a sort of irritation where it's like I owe something to this work. And I think there's a similar thing that I wanted to talk about in terms of other people's preoccupations with rhyme and form, and one example of that is some sort of story around Pound, right, where one of Pound's lifelong and I'm you know, I have really long engagement with Pound—for my sins, I guess—but one of his things that bugged him his entire life and he kept going back to was the poem by Guido Cavalcanti, the friend of Dante's in the *dolce stil nuovo*, and it's called "Donna mi prega." And people probably know some of this stuff, but the *dolce stil nuovo* was kind of the Italian adaptation of troubadour poetry, which was in Provençal and then was so influential and popular that it spread into the different vernaculars and by way of the so-called Sicilian school was adopted into Italian poetry. And Cavalcanti was Dante's friend. And then they kind of had a split. Dante puts his dad in the Inferno, it's a bummer.

But this poem is a truly incredible adaptation of troubadour lyric with super intricate metrics and also the presentation of a really weird sort of medieval Aristotelian-Aquinasian-Albert-the-Great psychology. It's a perfect example of *trobar clus*. So Pound, who said, "to break the pentameter, that was the first heave"—one of the major innovators of open form in English, it's one of the reasons, you know, like Basil Bunting said about the *Cantos*, "They are the Alps, fools!" You know, you can't get away from Pound. I definitely can't. And yet this poet who is so dedicated to hearing the musicality in each line of open form and always making it new, also always went to this particular poem, and not just this one, troubadour poetry in general, intricate forms. He would translate them and kind of come up with, frankly, bad translations.

And I'm a fan of Pound, but they're bad because he's trying to he's going through the training paces of, like, doing the rhymes in a language that's not Italian and doing the meter. And so they come up very stilted because they're apprentice exercises. Like his favorite translation of Dante was by this guy, Laurence Binyon. I don't know if anybody's ever followed that down from reading Pound, but it's basically unreadable because he does *terza rima* and it doesn't—no *terza rima* has ever worked in English, it just doesn't work.

So anyway, Pound was obsessed with this poem. He translated it dedicatedly. He edited a whole edition of Cavalcanti's works, which came out, I think, under Mussolini probably. And then he incorporated a portion of "Donna mi prega," into Canto 37, I think, which is: "A lady asks me, I speak in season"—super beautiful. So he was really obsessed with that. And that sets up this funny *agon* that happens between him and Louis Zukofsky, which is like a super sort of

Oedipal *agon* where Zukofsky has to take on "Donna mi prega" and do it better than Pound.

And maybe some people know the story, but this is where "A"–9 comes from, if anybody is familiar with that—the movement of "A," Zukofsky's long poem. The form of "A"–9 is the form of "Donna mi prega." But instead of talking about how love operates according to Aristotelian affect psychology, you know, Zukofsky famously makes it about Marx and makes a version of it that comes straight out of *Capital, Volume 1*—and not only that, but has all this intricate mathematics about conic sections in it, where conic sections govern the placement of certain letters, you know, which is totally a sort of topping Pound thing.

So that poem goes:

> An impulse to action sings of a semblance
> Of things related as equated values,
> The measure all use is time congealed labor
> In which abstraction things keep no resemblance
> To goods created; integrated all hues
> Hide their natural use to one or one's neighbor.
> So that were the things they could say: Light is
> Like night is like us when we meet our mentors
> Use hardly enters into their exchanges,
> Bought to be sold things, our value arranges;
> We flee people who made us as a right is
> Whose sight is quick to choose us as frequenters,
> But see our centers do not show the changes
> Of human labor our value estranges.

26:13

So that's the first sonnet section of "A"–9, which I wanted to memorize to see what would happen to it in the process of memorizing it. And of course one of the things that happens is you start to hear the internal rhymes and things that on the page look like Zukofsky or look like Cavalcanti. But when you say them it sounds like the internal rhymes in hip-hop, obviously, which is pretty cool. But so the "A"–9 thing was bugging me for a while and I kind of threw in something in my book called *The Ordinary*, which Michael Cross put out, which sort of fructified in a weird way from that, which is the last section called "To Romans."

And "To Romans" isn't exactly formally modeled on those works, but it takes a certain inspiration of constraint from them also in terms of translating an unpromising text, which in this case is Paul's letter to the Romans, a New Testament text—back to Romans, the Agamben connection. So I made, you know, using different constraints, this text and I'll just add that each section is a chapter from Romans, which has sixteen chapters. So I'll just read a little so you can get the flavor of it.

28:10

Paul apostle and Paul the slave
separate to good news of Christ
who sprang foretold from David's flesh
but god's son by the force of breath
through whom our undeserved grace
so that obedience by faith
might come to rule among the goys.
For my witness to you is god
I pray to come to teach his force
to save by faith that shows his right –
the <u>righteous</u> <u>live</u> <u>by</u> <u>faith</u> was writ.   Hab. 2:3
but shamelessness calls down his wrath
on those who work to hold back truth.
Their darkened hearts altered his fame
to rotten icons ; to their hearts then
what they wished : he gave them death.

## on Rhyme

Chapter two.

> Beware who judge against his right –
> can you escape judgment of god?
> Do you despise the wealth of grace?
> Your hardened heart is hoarding wrath.
> For life's to those who seek his fame
> by staying within works of force.
> But wrath's to those faithless to truth!
> Who lawless sin, lawless find death,
> but having law, thus judged. There's goys
> who lack law but work it from heart
> while their mind testifies to faith.
> God knows it when he sees through Christ.
> If you think you teach truth to slaves
> but blaspheme <u>God's name</u> as was writ,    Is. 52:5
> no benefit is your cut flesh –
> true circumcisions by the breath.

So that's two sections of the sixteen from "To Romans." And it's a formal adaptation and it's a translation from the Greek, and I worked through the Greek carefully to arrive at that metrical translation and also a translation that has determined end-words.

So in some ways, it's inspired by a sestina tradition that comes out of Provençal poetry—and those end-words are words that I found in Paul. So it was a way of thinking through the text of Paul formally; that is to say that, and this is something that I sort of began to perceive from reading secondary works about Paul, is that there are just these different trope-words that have a poetic or rhetorical function, they continuously appear—these thematic concerns. And people who have ever spent time with those texts will know it's a short list, it's like "the flesh," "grace," "the law," these kinds of words.

And I was like, you know, sort of that there's an immanent form in Paul that could be brought out formally to show how these concerns reappear and resequence in a work and sort of therefore have an internal thematic rhyme, you know, and it's not that the sonic rhyme that we that we think of when we think of end-rhyme, but that was like one step towards thinking about how rhyme could work in writing.

And I wanted to read just a short poem from this book I wrote that I never read from in New York called *Yo! Eos*. (Eos is the god of the dawn.) And I wrote this in 2010. And I guess what I'm thinking about here and in all my work and the work I want to read tonight, it's like, you know, I will write stuff that rhymes sometimes as exercise or to get it out of the head, but sometimes it's tuning.

And this is what I connect with Pound and to a certain degree with Zukofsky, somebody who doesn't really write in rhyme except for this one crazy virtuosic instance. And there's all kinds of poets like that, like Rod Smith gave me the new volume of the selected Creeley letters. And in those letters, Creeley is talking about rhyme. You know, you don't think about Creeley as somebody who's just, like, concerned with rhyme. And at the beginning of it, he's like, this rhyme works in Yeats.

Whereas if it was, you know, if this was Pope, it would be totally lifeless, and this kind of stuff. So it's like even the poets who we think of as not interested in rhyme, not even interested in closed form, are continuously thinking about the methods and the stakes of closed form in order to arrive at an open form that could actually be alive, like as alive as it can be through a saturation of the methods of closed form, I guess is what I mean.

And so I've been just thinking about that a lot as somebody who comes to poetry, as I think most people do now, from different kinds of open form and free verse traditions, to continue to have it be alive on the level of the line, in terms of the prosody of a line or a syntagm or whatever, the smallest units—to look at the resources that can be alive from closed forms in order to animate the open forms.

You know, and I think that's what a lot of people— Duncan also writes, you know, sort of rhyming poetry, O'Hara, you know, somebody else who people don't usually think of as writing rhyming poetry—early in his career, he has all this rhyming poetry. It's mostly goofy, of course, but, you know, O'Hara doesn't need rhyme to be goofy. So there's all kinds of poets who you don't think of as having this concern who do.

So I guess I want to read this and some of the things I'll read further on, to see how some of this stuff enters into work that's not primarily driven by rhyme. So this is just a short poem from *Yo! Eos*. It's "1.4.2010."

> "I was one of the
> crowd," I got
> peninsular, went
> west & now
> (the city to my right)
> blue vans pass,
> I wake up late & ask
> "what's work," to-
> day's, compromised by
> time and verbs that I
> don't know the way to
> plumb, froth of

33:09

> cloud crests flocked
> green hill to left &
> you get shadows, light-
> effects I notice here but
> "has the world changed or
> have I changed," power-lines,
> reflections, plants, the
> window, retrievals out of
> passing flows that we
> lay up, fished out &
> bleached by what befalls
> 'em, "metre-making
> argument" the
> woven script of it,
> rotated billboards &
> the thought of
> spirit, sun comes
> through this window &
> kicks off economy,
> all burgeons under-
> neath his auspices,
> if it's "his," (it
> aint), but habit's
> Ahriman (R.D.), the
> frozen men to serve as
> our dumb sentries.
> No reentries.

So that's from *Yo! Eos*, and it was like the fortuitous discovery that maybe that poem wanted to end on a rhyme, which is how some of this stuff happens.

And I wanted to read just as a thematic thing that doesn't involve sound or end-rhyme, and also because I was asked to read a little bit from this book, *Holy Ghost*, a piece that is about song and the reappearance of song. So this is from "Holy Ghost VIII."

## on Rhyme

There was a job to do in
America, communicant with
suffering of the father so
high in a rented bathroom, next
the shades, with infinite griefs of the
human heart laid amongst its befallments,
my father plaied,
my father, his
instruments inoperative like
schedules of sacrifices in the
house of death, go to
that infinite night, go
back, the body transduces all
woes to remind us, & your
real is this parcel so
narrow but
communicant, you
take a tiny number     of them out
of this life in your hand,
the hand that's dreamed out of your earthly hand.
The earthly liturgy.

And yeah, I think there's just the figure of the spiritual double or the twin that really preoccupies me in many ways and not just in poetry.

So one of the reasons I really wanted to talk about rhyme with you all is that I've done different kinds of writing work this year, and one of the projects that I finished is a book called *Gloriola*, and *Gloriola* is a book that involves a lot of rhyme. It's all rhyming. And I found my way into this territory to some degree unexpectedly, but through the experience of being an artist, of the necessity of fidelity to a direction, however, like, kinky, basically, that you got to go where it goes and this is the place where it wanted to go. And I don't necessarily think that I am going to live here, you know, continuously, but I wanted to really think about it, and I also wanted to think about poets of the tradition who I guess like—yeah, poets who had the choice and the chance not to use rhyme and did it anyway, which would be somebody like Yeats who definitely could have done another kind of writing, and also I just spent a lot of time thinking about Emily Dickinson and my sense of her place as obviously beloved and paid lip service to but in some degree also not getting her due in a certain way.

And so I was thinking about her work and reading her poetry exhaustively and being really amazed by the things I discovered in it that I wasn't expecting from reading the canon of her work. You know, one of many things that struck me were that not all of her poems are in ballad meter. You know, we all learn "Because I could not stop for Death, he kindly stopped for me," and that kind of poetry, it's very regular. Those are the anthology pieces. And they say, oh, you know, she learned this from Isaac Watts' hymnal in church and this kind of stuff. And she tweaked it and that's her aesthetic insight or whatever.

And in fact, her work is metrically much crazier than that. That's just one place in her metrical being. And it's like a place from which she can wander, which goes back to what I was trying to say before about people who sort of train in closed form or something in order to tone, in order to train their pitch, something like that, back to the Pound–Zukofsky thing.

And I really saw and felt like Dickinson, you know, really does that, too. And there is all of this work that is in different meters, meters that she probably made up—and also no kind of meter at all, you know, which is, you know, pretty wild, especially given the time of writing. And I also perceived something I had never really seen before, which is her connection with George Herbert and his book, *The Temple*, which is of course one of the great forebears of the serial poem, it's kind of the original serial poem maybe. And it's the sort of great religious poem that sort of, you know, the body of the poem creates the shape of a church. It's a great devotional poem in English. And it's really clear how much she got from Herbert.

And there's a really charming story, I think it's a really interesting, symptomatic story, where in the early process of the publication of her work, because obviously she wasn't around to supervise it, I believe Mabel Loomis Todd published a fragment from the famous box that later it was revealed was actually a poem of Herbert's.

And it had passed as an Emily Dickinson poem because it was so much like Emily Dickinson and not until some Herbert scholar would be like, oh, that's Herbert, you know? So it's a wonderful example of a certain kind of drag, like a transhistorical drag, and rhyme, you know. Their work was of such intimacy that the proximity became a formal one between, you know, the spirits of the poets of infinity. And of course, also the big thing for me to discover is like how very profoundly and however heterodoxly a religious poet and a Christian poet Dickinson is, which, you know, I guess probably people know that or something, but it had never really sunk in for me like that. She is just obsessed with, like, the resurrection and all of these Christian themes. And she's not just writing. You know, I think this is what I think about when

## A Talk

I think about the condescension to Dickinson. And in part, it's because she's a woman. And that's just like a chronic outcome of our misogynist society and patriarchal society, and that probably won't change until the patriarchy changes. But in addition to that, I think that there's the idea of her as the hermit and all of this kind of stuff. And I think in a way like a bit of a naïf, you know, almost like an outsider artist or like she kind of figured it out, patching things together, and this lack of willingness to grant her aesthetic, you know, the kind of aesthetic decision that we are willing to let other kinds of artists have.

So anyway, I wrote *Gloriola* in the process of thinking about a lot of that stuff, reading her and reading other work. So, yeah, there's definitely some ballad meter kind of stuff in here, but other things, too, just like in Dickinson. So I'm going to read some of these poems from *Gloriola*, which is a Latin word that means a little bit of glory.

41:51

> O song how shall I pay the rent
> O sun how shall I eat
> And shall I get back what I spent
> On whiles and winds and wheat
>
> O bird how shall I pay the tithe
> O day what shall I sell
> To have enough to feed myself
> And some for you as well
>
> O friend show me another law
> Than cash the king of all
> And I shall go to service there
> When I have heard the call.

\*

## on Rhyme

Sunday's name is
resurrection if you're
watching light,

electric lines will
bow beneath
the same old crows at night.

Had I but a scintilla I
would show you what I know,

In times like these
With no degrees
It's time for me to go.

I asked the animal and said:
What would you have me say?

He was too wise to make replies
So I wrote down today.

One corbie & one corbie
Is sitting in the tree
Life enough this morning
And death enough for me.

\*

When for a song like birdsong we are praying in the light,
as if to be the ones becoming graces in your sight,
we know we wont arrive at song or law without a fight.

\*

Two birds and the resurrection come,
Listen for the trumpet and the drum

Listen for the signal and then heed it
Ask the Lord for grace because you'll need it

Ask the day tell me what is your favor
Ask for strength cause otherwise you'll waver

Ask the light to nuance its surprises
Ask the earth if it knows what what dies is

Ask the sidewalk who has it seen stepping
Ask the wind whose fortune it's been repping

Ask your sons and daughters shall you love me
Ask the heaven how's it look above me

Ask fortuna shall I have more chances
Ask the stars when shall they cease their dances

Ask the smoke if it is borne off where
Ask the saint ought we be without care

Ask the sun what will tomorrow bring
Ask the grave o death where is thy sting

So those are a few from *Gloriola*, and what I think I would like to do is close with a newer poem that I wrote this month, last week, which I would love to read to you all and I think will be thematically related, and then maybe use the rest of whatever time we have together to just have more of a conversation since it sounds like there are some questions and I would relish the chance to talk about this stuff with you all.

So, yeah, I'm just going to read one more poem and I wrote this October 9, apparently, and it is called "Alcatraz Avenue," which is a street in Oakland, California. So, "Alcatraz Avenue."

43:32

Out the corner of my eye I
elegize a house that looks no different
than its neighbors when in transit,

## on Rhyme

ghost of my removéd sprezzatura when in
sunshine dustroom or the
lust of eyes, a picture how the most calm
Antioch of sighs might issue out of
toast dry toast for breakfast once again in
poverty of grappa for my forebears,
scrappers everyplace who hoisted up
the rusted-through-them frames of fridges out
our domiciles say or make a future route to
action by a clearing, so the letter's
open giving pour to aria you'll
get to later in the record, do the
grapevine twist & ask yourself by
George what troth is this & to what
commune, to what color of a heaven if it's
endless Oakland blue with salt of wit, a
torrid solar paradigm you cant get used to,
signalling by hand for ancillary superstars to
get they ass here pronto, so, it's all like
how ya gonna pay for this here rodeo when
all our money crashed & took the back door out
while we were dealing in your friend the
one with the bad eye, not so irreprehensible
as you said in your texts & can I take you up
on that smoke bath you promised me & free
alleviation from the counterplot my vexéd
second cousin. Ask the kids they'll lead you
down to alchemy & loiter there the intersection of
perfection where you think you'll be forever so
enjoy that rollie.  Could be light pours into
cups of tea that taste like cake a minute
longer no way through it but by bike hop on they
never steal the aqua ones in Ithaca or Oakland,
right.  Have pie, we serve it daily in my
commie coffee shop at every hour you can make
fantastic conversations furnishing a contour of
your every future in a mind at least wherever
that is in a language say & what rolls out of
that, the image. Some will salt & some will light.
In Felpham's vale a pidgin gets you up the

# A Talk

ladder where the angels sit dispensing
song from etymology, and I wont wed death no
matter how you pay me, I am taken. If you'll
retrain insouciance directed to the
sun of justice I like all my holy children feed on
saved-up light. A mandala repeats itself in
every place a poet lives around a glass or
house because we will not die. We just pull
strands of wool & linen out the body for forever for our
garments aint no matter what the motherfuckers say, &
aint that right, & aint that true, & aint that
what the lady said my sister called Sophia of the
blues. In her endostyle's map of priestly blessing like
a dandelion fruit goes anyplace & prills will
bear it to the furthest provinces of all
the princes of the visage, to the
nations we could tabulate for our ecologies of
song again, the thing that travels like
commodity, these clothes, a name for it, the
work that vanishes to made, so prim in its
obscurity of duct. Deal me in &
let me ride that figured
equine with an adze till principles of
our mimesus melt forever o my bandmates,
asking for a salve for spindled times, the
clearing of the rubbish calls for endless dumpruns &
who pays, who binds the generations with a
little thread of words who finds the
basis for our via in the graveyard of the
homicides in Oakland for this year that
multiplies like mushrooms after rain.
Say then that a dove has sent you. Then what. How
do you spell Gibreel inside your
argot, my Spinozist? Get some
jerky for your phratry,
this here T-shirt's about had it,
meantime all the previews are like
pharaohs you could
be. Take to me the subject fact'ry wash
me in the water and I'll wade within the water I will

## on Rhyme

wade to be baptized. A colophon. A bunch of
cranes. And don't forget to stop. An
inflorescence of these flowers on an
axis us my mates,
a little bit of middle pain we
gather from abandonment which is like
is it welt or is it what has fallen from
the spirit shedding predicates like
dirt from a construction washed away in
rain, if we got rain. An enemy waits crouching
at the feast to testify who did you feed who
did you turn away. His name is Dumah, now
you know. I heard it in a whisper so I
say it in a whistle. Gather forces for the
warfare, build the forms, remember its
mortality by brethren anyone will be your
aid to human fallibility like mirrors. This
will be side one, it will have been forever
& you still rampage across this
desert made of glass. The point of
contact is the circuit that the infinite
can make with time without explaining it,
or anything.

I tell time by the shade shop clock,
I wake up waiting for the short sharp shock.

This is the coronation of
Alcatraz Avenue, a radius of
burial a bundle of his,
where we flourish out from the
radicle of death a dove her
house the answer at the foot,
and really one picture if you
saw it from space, & I may
say whose body is a
saturate of evidence implasticized to
resonate it, Antioch America the
realistic Christ which
emphasizes moral choice of

vehicle an Acura Impala a
Corolla, yeah, this
bumpkin in a midsize town is
just as loyal to his
fate as Job by grace the
spiders in the showers or
in insulation testify to
patience of a dwelling to
withdraw the very linen from
your body to make homes inside
the desolation of hard vacuum of
the right to cash for ones who are not us,
a forest treatise in the midst of
this direction within music proverbs
sing of Wisdom gendered
feminine & coming now from
where she sits at
spindle of creation just to tell
how it should be
the story really starts, one
line that runs from
death into an
outlet at the head of a clear mountain,
where the mystic volumes shift by arrows to
enroll a traffic of the spirit beings coming
every morning from the river of the fire to
intone their wholly passing note, all right.
We unearth dice. We start to count
the mercy seat, we dictate lore
of iv'ry, check our
iceblink in albedo of the fatal
magnitudes of these our psychic settlements to
get back to a civic that's a rope between us,
there are scrappers everyplace to haul out
the debris from private houses I cant recognize,
their windows are opacities of gaze that
makes the moral field we live in everyday,
the shadows of the fronds make their decisions as to
what I'll dream, I wanted to say what it was like in
summer but nobody knows anymore, but that a

## on Rhyme

sapphire entered my flesh in forever like a lighted
vapor making me to suffer its couvade as love will
do according to its law, and now I will to
shift my gears when it is not a downhill stretch to
make a circuit of connection with the linen & the
wool like spiders will in homes or insulation,
play it as it lays but it will still turn out, the
card the die the game of sticks will yield a
face of that determination which you are &
then from there you're dwelling in a
picture of a compound curve & asking every
day what is the further work and answer,
really every very flesh can cast a shadow here, the
pelican can meet Saint Paul or Augustine under
repairs, a tourniquet will answer it a
grass will grow upon intentions right. Like which
the battle that would intermit. So floating
light above the shoal of turbid present
matter kneads a dough of answer that
suffices must suffice a
basketweaver me. My avenue is
only how you get there. Light of
course and plenty of trees. The
mystic volumes. Traffic till you're
dead. Salt in a jar. The circles &
circuits, the cycles & spiders, the
pacts & permissions, the communes &
commons, the dead in their bundles,
the wind in its wander,
bare feet on easter,
among the cypress in a tiny park together by the
mountains clear the mountains underneath the overpass where
they're still building
whatever replaces the safeway.

Thank you. And what I would like to do if folks want to do this is maybe just take a limited number of questions like, I don't know, three or something that could be viewed as an extension of the talk. And then we can sort of formally adjourn so the folks who want to scoot, scoot, but I can hang out if people want to talk more informally about it. So I don't know if there are folks who have questions that they might like to have a thinking in public version?

> Question 1 [James Sherry]: *So I get the impulse for closed form especially in the context of globalization, in the context of an environmental environmentally challenged planet where everything seems to be impacted by the same issues of information as a model for all thought, no matter whether you're in China or in New York, and it seems like a very interesting way, as you say, rhyme to get from those kinds of issues to a political form, and that's how you translate. I think that's pretty interesting. And I also like the things that you've said in favor of rhyme, not for what I just said, that the as you said, they agree on. But what I didn't hear and I'd like to hear more about are how you address the reasons why people moved away from rhyme, such as these or others, the closed form being anti-democratic, closed form missing out on the diversity of people, those political issues, or in the sense of, let's say, Language Poetry, where there's a whole range of prosodic conventions that could be addressed and pushed as meaning rather than focusing on a single totalizing one. And I said, why I understand that impulse, so, you know, the political, the prosodic, or the way in which you undercut the New York school idea of common speech, which was instituted all sorts of, you know, political or or institutional critique. And what and how do you feel about those reasons why people*

*left rhyme rather than sticking with it and trying to change?*

DB: Totally. And that's a great question or field of questions or sort of nodes of things to think about.

And as I said, like most people my age, I came up on a lot of this kind of stuff and open form stuff in general. And then, of course, the various sort of avant-gardes that have worked with different kinds of innovations in form. So that, in a way, is the first thing, you know, or one of the first things I came to as a writer. But one of the things I'm interested in is I guess something like trying to complicate the question between closed form and plain speech, which I think is like a long-standing rift in American poetry that replays itself out, Heraclitus and Parmenides style, with different kinds of figures where, you know, you can think about, you know, Whitman and Dickinson as like plain speech versus hermetic.

And that plays out again with like Pound and Williams. And, you know, we could probably play this game all night. But I think that it's an interesting nuance that in different ways in terms of what the people who are apparently the boosters for, say, plain speech—like Whitman is an example that I think about a lot because of and this connects with the democratic thing in some ways and with the folk tradition, because, you know, I've really been interested in where does, you know, open form and free verse actually come from, you know, and there's various narratives and genealogies.

And of course, practitioners put together their own elective affinities. And those can become very persuasive stories like, you know, we come up on like Eliot's version, where it comes from France or something. But in fact, you know, there's a really profound tradition in English poetry that comes from different resources. One of them is the Hebrew Bible and the language and the poetry of the Psalms and the prophets, because they didn't really necessarily understand how the poetry worked.

And it has a structural principle—back to the beginning of the talk—it's just not rhyme. It's parallelism, which is characteristic of Semitic poetry. But because this wasn't understood or perfectly understood, people adapted it as though it was free. So there's a misunderstanding of a form. It's like one of the places where free verse comes from, sort of for Whitman, also for Christopher Smart. But more to the point of what you're bringing up is Whitman's debt to the ballad tradition.

And, you know, Whitman is on record as saying that he owned and was obsessed with Sir Walter Scott's collection of border ballads and Scott's minstrelsy, which is this, you know, sort of before the sort of big collection of Frances James Child, which is the sort of definitive collection of those kinds of ballads, most of which end up, you know, inform the American musical tradition and are recorded on things like the Harry Smith *Anthology of American Folk Music*. Whitman was obsessed with that stuff.

And that's all closed. You know, it's obviously it's ballad meter, it's the folk tradition. So I think it's just interesting to see how there's like a certain kind of music that that comes from a folk culture that is taken on as explicitly democratic and that has a closedness to it. And I think that my personal appropriation of this, I guess, and of course, like this is really open work for me. You know, you're seeing, like, the things that I'm thinking about right now, I don't have any sort of finished aesthetic statement to say about this stuff.

But in a way the experience of 2011 and Occupy Oakland for me and Occupy in general changed a lot of people's writing in a way. And certainly where I live, it's generally agreed upon that people's writing was really changed by that moment in different ways. And I feel like for me, one of the basic ways that it was actually changed is in terms of diction and the desire to move towards poetry that would potentially be more legible, so therefore the double task of how to remain faithful to aesthetic perception while also attempting to create a poetry that is actually more legible, not pandering, but also not all *trobar clus*, which goes towards the sort of question of a democratic poetry.

And of course, that's the open question of address and reception. There's only so much you can do. And I wouldn't you know, it's not my desire to pander in the hope that more people would read this poetry, because that's obviously a fairy tale. But, you know, just in terms of the moment, it's less about actual reception and more about what seems to want to come, like, out of my body, basically. And it's kind of that. So I don't know, that's an attempted answer or response to some of those things.

> Question 2 [Farnoosh Fathi]: *Thanks so much, David, this has been so inspiring, I really appreciate it, and I guess my question has to do with, um, I guess the relationship for you between consciousness*

*and rhyme. And specifically I'm thinking in terms
of function both as something that allows for sense
to be made. You know, things like Stein saying being
intelligible is not what it seems. So what's rhyme's
role in intelligibility? And once it becomes—is its
function recognition of sense, meaning like if I am
participating in a purely oral tradition whereby
rhyme allows me to shape sense, make sense, transmit sense, preserve sense, then when I'm the recipient
of that and I'm acculturated to that form, then I recognize it both as a signifier of poetry, but also as a sort
of aesthetic element.*

*So at what point does the relationship between
aesthetics of rhyme and function of rhyme become a
fiction of form? So if you think of like the individual
word and the phrase—Josephine Miles studying, say,
Whitman, a phrasal poet, as opposed to Dickinson,
a clausal poet. Someone who is a phrasal poet is,
in her mind, someone with a predisposition toward
the sublime, whereas a clausal poet is discursive and
maintains a discursive ground base. So if that's a
fiction of form and then you think about closed form,
sonnets, and the notion that they lend themselves
towards the portrayal of, say, like an emotional relationship, like the course of a relationship through
the various emotions and ups and downs of an affair.
So I guess my question is, you know, putting open
and closed aside, what are the sort of fictions of form
that this notion of rhyme elicits for you? You know,
is it something like, because, you know, anything
that's a construct, anything that's generative, which
rhyme is, and preservative, is going to have its fiction. I don't know what your opinion is, but I feel*

*like n+7 or whatever constraint—a lipogram—has as much of a fiction in terms of what it produces, it's like, oh, this doesn't make sense, it's got an absurdist element, because of the particular constraint. So putting aside the open and closed debate, where does the fiction of form relate to rhyme for you?*

DB: Totally. And of course, again, a question that's like a field I could, like, walk across. And there's a lot of cool objects in the field.

But I guess the first thing that occurs to me to say is this really great line from a letter of Hölderlin's where he writes to a friend and he says, "The most difficult thing is the free use of the proper." And it could also be translated "the free use of one's own" or also "the free use of the national." You know, it just depends how you translate the German in question. And I'm really interested in that ambiguity, that ambiguity and situation of address.

And I bring that up, I think, in light of your question and also, James, this question and think about something like the propriety of grace in use, which is to say, can you pick up and use the relevant instrument? Can something very binding be meaningful within the use of a larger space of freedom of creation? And I think that in the history of literature, one of the things that I'm most preoccupied with is emergence of genre, moments of generic emergence and the kind of de-reification of genre.

Like in school we learned, you know, this is what an elegy is. This is what an ode is. This is what a play is—this is what a *poem* is. You know what I mean? And if you go back to the earliest strata of these traditions, you find out—we know what a play is. We read a Greek play, and we're like, oh, it's a play.

It's not a play. It's like a civic ritual, it's a religious rite, and it's also some kind of aesthetic object. But to just say, oh, yeah, we know what that is, that's a play, is to radically distort the thing and our ability to understand it, and therefore also our ability to learn how to innovate out of the innovations of the past. I mean, I think about this a lot also reading Dante, which, you know, I'm really preoccupied with and sort of always doing, and of course, Dante's obviously one of the hoariest figures of a canon, right. Like *the* canon. And yet Dante was this very serious architect of originary form, originary form coming out of the traditions that preceded him, but becoming such a profound architect of a new thing out of those things that it seems totally sovereign in his gesture, you know what I mean? So, like, he picks up aspects of Provençal culture and even, of course, includes Provençal poetry in the *Comedy*. But he picks up a sort of *canzone*, a sort of modified *canzone* form for the cantos of the *Comedy*.

And he learns from those intricate schemes to innovate his own scheme of *terza rima*, which of course now is very familiar from Dante. But, you know, he made that up and it was like the thing that solved his issue, which was formal and radically transcendent of the formal for his needs, including a temporal model like the temporal model of the sestina, that Agamben talks about, a religious and theological model, and a model of forward movement through time where the *terza rima*—actually one of the beautiful things about the *Comedy* is that it's so limpid in the writing that you can easily not notice the *terza rima*.

## on Rhyme

It stands out sometimes, but it really works in Italian in a way that like sometimes he'll have to bring in some weird word to make it work and then you'll be like, well, that's obviously brought it for the rhyme, the way rhyme often works, but there's whole passages where you won't. And I feel like maybe this is a way of signaling towards how I think you opened your question, which is sort of like rhyme and consciousness or rhyme and life, and that's something that I'm really super interested in and not necessarily super able to be articulate about, except to gesture towards a lifelong interest in divination and in practices in antiquity and in the present concerning how to read the world in different ways and how to read coincidence and how to read these things as rhymes.

And there's various more and less credible ways to do this, basically, depending upon what your episteme validates as a hermeneutics. So we live in a sort of super, you know, secularized capitalist episteme that says, like, this shit is real and all this shit is not real.

But obviously this is one episteme successive upon other ones and it will be succeeded by yet other ones. So while we're living through this, I'm really interested in what are the through lines, like even the through lines, through this dreadful and fatal episteme that are going to carry us through the other side, and to me, those are like the rhymes in the *Comedy*, like the rhymes that you don't catch, like we're walking through them every day and we can be more and less attuned to them.

But they're all actually happening, like, ontologically and, you know, like, yes, I'm a kook. It's fine. I don't mind, you know. So is that OK? OK, cool. Yeah. Maybe one more?

Question 3 [Brenda Iijima]: *Just tracing your trajectory as a poet, it feels like instinctually subject matter and form are now really bonding in a deep way with your work, and it seems like the rhymes are instigating this religiosity or attention to the spiritual in a way that I hadn't seen in your work before, which has always been about quotidian perception and, like you say, negotiating the daily in a way that's hyper-sensitive and allowing as many balances into your practice or your attention as possible, but now as well, in addition, I also see all of these things playing in, but I also see this very exact attention toward the precepts of Judeo-Christian belief saturating the social-political space, and I just wonder how you would speak about that, how the subject matter became this thing that now has grown into this magnitude, this proportion that—you're using the New Testament as a filter for Marx or your political activism or even your tonality of voice or how I even hear you as a person, how your affect is now morphing or being re-energized through these very specific battles.*

DB: Sure. Yeah. Well, you know, I am a Christian and I'm an adult convert, so that conditions a lot of my recent writing for sure. And poetry and writing of all kinds have really been a way to help me understand that passage, basically.

And so I think that a lot of work has that concern, but has a concern with the complexity of that. And, you know, I love William Blake and Blake, who is a Christian. There were a lot of Christians out there.

## on Rhyme

You know, Martin Luther King was a Christian. Dorothy Day was Christian. Christopher Smart was a Christian. The list could go on and on. There's a lot of very interesting, strange, and heterodox people working through forms of Christianity that are also just super radical.

And so sometimes because people know my politics, they ask like, oh, how does your religious life comport with that stuff? I'm like, well, lucky for me, it says in the Acts of the Apostles all goods shall be in common. So, like, I'm fine, you know what I mean? It's not a problem.

So I think that the writing that I've done in recent years represents a working through of a lot of that stuff and just felt, subjective experience, because I still feel like there is an important role for writing to be a registration of subjective experience, otherwise invisible, but as it intersects with sort of the giant machines that are always chopping us all up. And I think, yeah, playing out sort of in terms of formal concerns. And I think about that in terms of the *Gloriola* writing, for example, and going into Dickinson, where I see like her real Jacob and the Angel wrestling with not only the sort of theological concerns of the tradition—she's coming out of a certain kind of Unitarianism, coming out of American Calvinism—but also what that looks like in terms of poetic practice, in terms of hymns and in terms of literary poetry proper and sort of getting what she was doing from the hymn tradition, getting all kinds of resources from it.

And just for me, connecting that as the great stream that that comes out in American popular music to going back to the theme and also the overture of the song—that generationally, you know, for me it seems clear that many people my age are obsessed with music but popular music. And a lot of it's like sort of abject mass-produced commodity music.

But where does that music actually come from? You know what I mean? The real origin of those traditions is the confluence of white Anglo-Scot balladry traditions, which carried the border ballads to America, usually through Appalachia, and African-American traditions, many of which preserve different aspects of sort of West African music, but which also very early on and very decisively take on and create music based on the Christian churches that were founded, you know, throughout America really early on, both in the South and in the North.

Those are the places where our music comes from. That's where soul comes from. Everybody knows this. But I don't think we think about it enough. This is what I mean about the river that's passing through our episteme, you know what I mean? That music is debased now, but maybe its form of being debased is a way for it to survive this catastrophe.

You know, I always think about this motif that shows up in a lot of Gnostic writing, *sophia*, you know, the sort of feminine principle of wisdom who was with God at the beginning of the creation according to the Book of Proverbs, sort of being cast into the world and, you know, more or less compelled to become abject in many cases, compelled to become a prostitute and all these kinds of things.

But she's like passing through this abjection in order to come out the other side and be wisdom again.

And so I guess being wisdom again is a perfectly fine place to adjourn. And thank you all for entertaining this.

And please come talk to me, I'd love to meet you if I haven't met you already.

# A Bibliography on Rhyme
and Related Issues

*A Talk on Rhyme* is a text distilled in 2021 from a talk given on October 17, 2014, for the Leslie Flint Series at Berl's Poetry Store in Brooklyn, New York, as the first in a series of occasional presentations on fundamental issues in poetry.

The talk, presented at the invitation of Jamie Townsend and introduced by Ian Dreiblatt, was conceived as a performance lecture, and in part as an experiment in orality and memory. Apart from the opening epigraphs from Giorgio Agamben and Jack Spicer, and my own poetry, the entire presentation was delivered extemporaneously and without notes over the course of about an hour. Through the fine hospitality of Farrah Field and Jared White, the proprietors of Berl's, who I here thank, the talk was recorded and preserved on the bookstore's website, where it remains at time of writing. At the suggestion of Phil Baber, publisher of the Yellow Papers pamphlet series, I set about transforming the 2014 recording into a 2021 text—reading what was never written. As part of this process, Phil suggested that I prepare a bibliography, and that is the text which you are reading right now.

It seems appropriate that Phil should have asked me for a bibliography, since he first became aware of my work through the essayistic bibliography I prepared for *Revolution: A Reader* (Lisa Robertson and

Matthew Stadler, eds.; Publication Studio, 2012). It's a book that never had much distribution in the US (my contributor's copy was the only one I ever saw), but it obviously had some interesting circulation in Europe. In that text, I was preoccupied with deepening and challenging the idea of revolution by considering transformative moments in the full history of human beings as a species, including the emergence of art and writing as well as more recent developments like the printing press, without losing sight of the political urgency of revolutionary transformations in our social and economic life. Because of its concern with symbolic systems, there's some overlap between that text and this one. As Gertrude Stein is supposed to have said: *I do not repeat, I insist*.

The Berl's talk opens with "Rime is the Body of My Resurrection," a sonnet published in *Holy Ghost* (City Lights, 2017). The closer translates a verse from the first canto of Dante's *Paradiso*, which I like to read in the Modern Library rendition by Anthony Esolen. (Don't read Laurence Binyon's translation in *The Portable Dante* (Viking, 1953).) This line was around in my household because my now-ex-wife Sara Larsen had translated Canto I for a reading we gave in San Francisco in 2010, the year my father died. (I had translated *Paradiso* XIV, on the resurrection of the body.) Thinking about rhyme is always thinking about history, and Dante's work is an inescapable part of poetry's progress. One of the few volumes that survived my cross-country move from Oakland to New Orleans was the blue-bound one-volume *Commedia* (C. H. Grandgent, ed.; D. C. Heath and Company, 1933). Its bookmark is a postcard of

## on Rhyme

Domenico di Michelino's painting *Dante e il suo Poema*, purchased at the Duomo where the original painting is on view, and signed on the back by me, Sara, Anne Winters, and Julian Talamantez Brolaski the night we finished a years-long project of reading the text of the poem in Italian, sitting in the apartment on Alcatraz Avenue. "well, my window / looked out on the Squero where Ogni Santi / meets San Trovaso / things have ends and beginnings" (from Canto LXXVI of Ezra Pound's *Cantos* (New Directions, 1995)).

The book about Dante I've gone back to with greatest frequency is John Freccero's *Dante: The Poetics of Conversion* (Harvard, 1988), which among other riches has a fine essay on the philosophical and theological meanings of the poem's *terza rima* scheme. The relationship between Dante and Pound is studied in James Wilhelm's *Dante and Pound: The Epic of Judgment* (University of Maine, 1974).

My talk's first epigraph derives from Giorgio Agamben's *The Time That Remains: A Commentary on the Letter to the Romans* (Stanford, 2005), the reading of which I owe to a conversation with Chris Nealon in Juliana Spahr's backyard during the baby shower for her son Sasha, which was organized by Stephanie Young and Judith Goldman (another ex). Chris told me he had been teaching about the "Pauline turn"—a term that designated continental philosophy's attention to the texts of the apostle as evidenced in Agamben's book and other works like Alain Badiou's *Saint Paul: The Foundation of Universalism* (Stanford, 2003). I didn't know it at the time, but the study of Agamben's book, which I've read many times since, was an important nudge of the Holy Spirit toward my conversion to Christianity in 2013, and the undertaking of my pastoral vocation in 2015. So thanks Chris.

Agamben's book led me, as it has many others, to Jacob Taubes' *The Political Theology of Paul* (Stanford, 2003). This testamentary masterpiece is not only one of the great books about Paul, it is a penetrating meditation on Christianity, and on religion as a whole, at the end of the career (and the life) of one of the most fascinating scholars of the twentieth century. (This is what's known as a strong recommendation.) The study of these books forms the background for the series published as *To Romans*, first in a chapbook from Michael Cross's Compline Press, and subsequently in my first book, *The Ordinary* (Compline, 2013). I wrote those poems in December of 2011—midway between the police raids on Occupy Oakland and the baptism I didn't know was coming (though perhaps the writing was on the wall, as they say).

Taubes' book, as suggested by the title, is in dialogue with Carl Schmitt's *Political Theology* (University of Chicago, 2006), and in fact with Schmitt himself, who Taubes met as a young man. The junior, Jewish scholar explained his exegesis of the notoriously difficult ninth, tenth, and eleventh chapters of Romans to the older political philosopher, notorious for his support of the Nazi party, after which Schmitt exclaimed: "You must tell someone about this before you die!" Decades later, when Taubes received a terminal diagnosis, he immediately made plans to give the oral presentation whose transcript forms the book it is now possible for us to read.

Another important interlocutor in this conversation is Walter Benjamin, who corresponded with Schmitt

## on Rhyme

and whose influence on Taubes was in part mediated by Gershom Scholem. Agamben puts Paul's text in conversation with Benjamin's own testamentary document, the "Theses on the Philosophy of History," which were discovered in a briefcase after the critic's suicide in Port Bou, Spain. These texts and associated documents are conveniently available in volume 4 of Benjamin's *Selected Writings* (Michael Jennings and Howard Eiland, eds.; Belknap/Harvard, 2006). The student of these gnomic writings might benefit from reading Michael Löwy's *Fire Alarm* (Verso, 2006), a sort of *vade-mecum* to the texts and their place in the larger universe of Benjamin's writings. I'll also mention here that years of study as a non-academic autodidact have convinced me that despite the strip-mining of Benjamin's work in the humanities, his work remains too important to leave to the academics. Let them have Adorno.

Elsewhere in the *Selected Writings*, in "The Paris of the Second Empire in Baudelaire," Benjamin reports the anecdote of Flaubert's friend Maxime du Camp, famous for his history of Paris: "It suddenly occurred to [du Camp] ... that [Paris] too, the city bustling all around him, would have to die someday, the way so many capitals had died." The historical rhyme between the capitals of antiquity and nineteenth-century Paris, so important to Benjamin, came to my mind as I was reflecting on the view of the Transamerica Pyramid from my apartment in Oakland. The great book on the despoliation of the earth that it took to make San Francisco a world capital is Grey Brechin's *Imperial San Francisco: Worldly Power, Earthly Ruin* (University of California, 2006). A more recent meditation on the destruction of place wrought by tech money and real estate speculation is Richard Walker's *Pictures of a Gone City: Tech and the Dark Side of Prosperity in the San Francisco Bay Area* (PM Press, 2018). Not only did I sit in on Walker's long-running reading group for Marx's *Capital, Volume 1* (Penguin, 1992; read it), I even got to hear him sing Guillaume de Machaut at a church in Berkeley.

Oh gosh, David, when are you going to talk about rhyme? Well, what is rhyme? 2014 rhymes with 2021 now, and *that rhyme is historical* is the fundamental concern of both the talk, the *Talk*, and this bibliography. (Even rhyme in the classic, normative sense of terminal assonance is historical, since it's a function of phonology that emerges and changes in time, right?) And we don't get history without some dirt on the roots.

A question I discussed with Julian Brolaski many years ago, with which I am still preoccupied, is: *where does rhyme come from?* In the European context, it docs not exist in classical antiquity as a structural principle of verse, though it sometimes appears in the rhetorical feature called *homoioteleuton*—the Greek way of saying "similar ending." (The question of differing structural principles of verse across the poetry of the world was first brought to my attention in W. K. Wimsatt's *Versification: Major Language Types* (Modern Language Association, 1972), which builds off of the insights of Roman Jakobson in texts like *Six Lectures on Sound and Meaning* (MIT, 1978).) Rhyme appears, as though out of nowhere, in the words of the Provençal troubadours, whose work is best studied in the *en face* edition of Frederick Goldin, *Lyrics of the Troubadours and Trouveres* (Knopf, 1973). (The older anthology by Raymond Thompson Hill and

## on Rhyme

Thomas Goddard Bergin, *Anthology of the Provençal Troubadours: Texts, Notes, and Vocabulary* (Yale, 1941), as well as the standard three-volume collection by Martín de Riquer, *Los trovadores: historia literaria y textos* (Editorial Ariel, 1975), are also worth having, though neither of them present English translations.) The two prevailing hypotheses as to the source of rhyme are a mutation out of the medieval ("Vulgar") Latin tradition of verse and song, or a borrowing from the rhyming traditions of the near East. (Additionally, Lisa Robertson speculates on troubadour "rime" as a pure novum in her talk on "Wide Rime" preserved on the *If I Can't Dance* website, a presentation in dialogue with her chapbook *Starlings* (Krupskaya, 2017).) My studies have led me to conclude that Romance rhyme is a borrowing from the Arabic *muwashshah*, whose refrain (the *kharja*, often in Arabic but sometimes written in the hybrid Arabic-Romance dialect known as Mozarabic) features rhyme. This poetic form travelled from the Arabic-speaking Near East through cultural contacts which include both the Crusades and the Moorish culture of Andalusian Spain, which brought Arabic and Hebrew poetry and music into contact with Latin and Romance cultures of Christian Europe: specifically the Iberian peninsula and the region of what is now southern France where troubadour art first arose. The unique ferment of Andalusia is well-treated in Gil Anidjar's *"Our Place in al-Andalus": Kabbalah, Philosophy, Literature in Arab Jewish Letters* (Stanford, 2002), while the generative role of Arabic poetry in this hybrid cultural zone is lyrically sketched by Maria Rosa Menocal in her *Shards of Love: Exile and the Origins of the Lyric* (Duke, 1994), as well as her *Arabic*

*Role in Medieval Literary History* (University of Pennsylvania, 2004). As Anidjar's subtitle indicates, medieval Spain and Provence were also a seedbed of the Jewish mystical tradition, a genealogy taken up by Gershom Scholem's *Origins of the Kabbalah* (Princeton, 1987). The unique translinguistic texts of this epoch are studied by Alois Nykl in *Hispano-Arabic Poetry and its Relation with the Old Provençal Troubadours* (Furst, 1946) and by Samuel Miklos Stern in *Hispano-Arabic Strophic Poetry: Studies* (Oxford, 1974), and the *muwashshah* and *kharja* are treated in Linda Fish Compton's *Andalusian Lyric Poetry and Old Spanish Love Songs* (New York University Press, 1976) as well as Otto Zwartjes' *Love Songs from Al-Andalus: History, Structure, and Meaning of the Kharja* (Brill, 1997). Texts for these poems are collected in James Monroe's *Hispano-Arabic Poetry: A Student Anthology* (University of California, 1974), as well as in his collection with Benjamin Liu, *Ten Hispano-Arabic Strophic Songs in the Modern Oral Tradition* (University of California Press, 1989). A. J. Arberry's *Arabic Poetry: A Primer for Students* (Cambridge, 1965) remains a valuable collection for students of the classical poetic tradition that underlies the Andalusian efflorescence.

I began studying Greek with Brandon Brown in 2006, and subsequently Latin with a number of Bay Area poets, but it was after my father died in 2010 that I really began to deepen my commitment to linguistic investigation as part of my poetic practice. (One of the fruits of the subsequent decade of work is an unpublished manuscript entitled *profane hours*, which collects texts by thirty-six authors in ten languages.) As an Anglophone poet, I have found it necessary to study the whole history of English poetry, from *Beowulf* to Frank O'Hara and beyond—but the truth is that such study leads inevitably to other languages and literatures. The earliest "English" verse is written in a Germanic language unintelligible to modern English speakers; Chaucer is unthinkable without French models; Sir Thomas Wyatt openly acknowledged his debt to Petrarch and other Italian authors. Beyond this, the study of poetry and language leads us inevitably into what Prospero calls "the dark backward and abysm of time." Also, since language is the medium of my artmaking I want to understand it as fully as possible—the way painters understand paint. This means getting into the guts of how it works—phonology, prosody, grammar, syntax, and diction—and also where it comes from. English is one branch of the Indo-European language family distributed from Ireland to India (and subsequently, via colonialism, worldwide) by horse-riding nomads whose cultural complex can be reconstructed by comparative linguistics. (This is the incredible task undertaken by Emile Benveniste in his *Indo-European Language and Society* (University of Miami, 1973).) There is also a deep kinship in prosody across languages, as outlined by Calvert Watkins in his *Comparative Studies in Greek and Indic Meter* (Harvard, 1974) and, more engagingly, in *How to Kill a Dragon: Aspects of Indo-European Poetics* (Oxford, 2001). The reflex of Indo-European oral poetry in the verse of Homer is studied in Milman Parry's *The Making of Homeric Verse* (Oxford, 1971). Since modern poetic meters emerge out of the classical matrix, it's also worthwhile to study *The Meters of Greek and Latin Poetry* (James Halporn, Martin

Ostwald, and Thomas Rosenmyer, eds.; University of Oklahoma, 1980), as well as the more technical work of M.L. West: *Greek Metre* (Oxford, 1983) and *Ancient Greek Music* (Oxford, 1992). However, I would be very remiss in this parade of erudition to fail to recall the sage advice that Frank O'Hara gives regarding prosody, in "Personism: A Manifesto" (in *The Collected Poems* (University of California, 1995)): "if you're going to buy a pair of pants you want them to be tight enough so everyone will want to go to bed with you." In other words, the proof of the pudding is always in the eating. (O'Hara also wrote: "the *Brise marine* wasn't written in Sanskrit, baby"—a fact of which I regularly remind myself. (But it *was* written in French!))

All of this is to say that when I study poetry written in other languages, I try to learn as much as possible about the language, since much of what I most want to learn comes from the language itself, and particularly the micro-features—details of prosody, syntax, and the euphony that Sanskrit grammarians call *sandhi*.

So it was that I acquired a copy of William Paden's *Introduction to Old Occitan* (Modern Language Association of America, 1998) and studied with Julian Brolaski and Kit Schluter at the now-defunct Cafe Renaissance on Shattuck Avenue in Berkeley. (Occitan is what they call Provençal nowadays.)

This gets us back to Agamben because, in *The Time That Remains*, he performs a study on an Occitan sestina by Arnaut Daniel from which was derived the quotation that furnished my talk's first epigraph. This poet's work, also very important to Ezra Pound who treated it in his *Spirit of Romance* (New Directions,

1968), is collected in the Garland Library of Medieval Literature's *Poetry of Arnaut Daniel* (James Wilhelm, ed.; Garland, 1981). The Garland series provides the best English-language editions of essential medieval poets in several languages (including *The Poetry of the Sicilian School* (Frede Jensen, ed.; Garland, 1986) —a crucial link between the troubadours and Dante), but unfortunately they are almost all out of print and expensive. Borrowing privileges at a university library are probably your best bet. Agamben also discusses the work of troubadour poets in his *Language and Death: The Place of Negativity* (University of Minnesota, 1991) and *The End of the Poem: Studies in Poetics* (Stanford, 1999). Finally, the philosopher cites Marianne Shapiro's study of temporality in the Petrarchan sestina, *Hieroglyph of Time* (University of Minnesota, 1980). If you gotta read Petrarch, do it in Robert Durling's edition: *Petrarch's Lyric Poetry: The* Rime sparse *and Other Lyrics* (Harvard, 1976).

Translations of Friedrich Hölderlin have proliferated over the years, but my favorite remains the first one I ever got, *Hymns and Fragments* (Richard Sieburth, trans.; Princeton, 1984). The most complete edition of the poetry in English (with facing German), and therefore indispensable, is *Poems and Fragments* (Michael Hamburger, trans.; University of Michigan, 1967). I was lucky enough to find a hardcover ex-library copy under a table at a booksale in Kansas City in 2004, and have held on to it ever since. Poetological documents are available in *Essays and Letters on Theory* (Thomas Pfau, trans.; SUNY, 1987) and now in *Essays and Letters* (Charlie Louth and Jeremy Adler, trans.; Penguin, 2009). Valuable secondary essays on the poet's work are collected in *The Solid Letter: Readings of Friedrich Hölderlin* (Aris Fioretos, ed.; Stanford, 1999). Hölderlin is the most important European poet between Milton and Blake, and we still have not caught up with what he has to teach.

The talk's second epigraph comes from Jack Spicer, whom I still read in *The Collected Books* (Robin Blaser, ed.; Black Sparrow, 1975), though it has been editorially superseded by *My Vocabulary Did This to Me: The Collected Poetry of Jack Spicer* (Kevin Killian and Peter Gizzi, eds.; Wesleyan, 2008). Gizzi also edited *The House That Jack Built: The Collected Lectures of Jack Spicer* (Wesleyan, 1998), which bears reading next to the prose texts of Hölderlin. Their juxtaposition is no accident.

Ezra Pound's season of apprenticeship as a secretary to William Butler Yeats is recounted in James Longenbach's *Stone Cottage: Pound, Yeats, and Modernism* (Oxford, 1998).

The contemporary discourse on inoperativity (in French, *désœuvrement*) which Agamben takes up in *The Time That Remains* (with respect to Paul's use of the Greek verb καταργέω) and elsewhere in his work has its ultimate root in a text of George Bataille, "Letter to X, Lecturer on Hegel," collected in *The Bataille Reader* (Blackwell, 1997). Bataille writes: "If action ('doing') is—as Hegel says—negativity, the question arises as to whether the negativity of one who has 'nothing more to do' disappears or remains in a state of 'unemployed negativity'." ("X" is Alexandre Kojève, whose influential lectures were collected in his *Introduction to the Reading of Hegel* (Cornell, 1980).) The theme was subsequently taken up in Jean-Luc

Nancy's *Inoperative Community* (University of Minnesota, 1981) and Maurice Blanchot's *Unavowable Community* (Station Hill, 1988).

My "Hymn of the Twin in Prison" was published in *The Emerald Tablet* (Derek Fenner, ed.; Bootstrap, 2014). As far as I can recall, I translated it from the Syriac text published in Anthony Bevan's *Hymn of the Soul Contained in the Syriac Acts of St. Thomas* (Cambridge, 1897), though I don't have the book in front of me, or the photocopies I made from it, to confirm that this was the source. Other translations of this classic text may be found in anthologies of gnostic texts like Willis Barnstone's *Gnostic Bible* (Shambhala, 2003).

The Cambridge Poets series published a one-volume edition of Francis James Child's *English and Scottish Popular Ballads* (Houghton Mifflin, 1904); that's the one I have, though I'll spare you its gruesome provenance. A five-volume paperback reprint with variants was published by Dover in 1965—a press which, along with Harper Torchbooks, is one of the autodidact's best friends. Greil Marcus' *Invisible Republic* (Holt, 1997), a study of Harry Smith's *Anthology of American Folk Music* (Smithsonian, 1997) and Bob Dylan's *Basement Tapes* (Columbia, 2014), digs deep into the traditional roots of American popular music and it's fun to read.

Emily Dickinson? I'm sure you already know to read Susan Howe's *My Emily Dickinson* (North Atlantic, 1985) and "These Flames and Generosities of the Heart: Emily Dickinson and the Illogic of Sumptuary Values," collected in *The Birth-Mark* (University Press of New England, 1993). The author's religious background is well laid-out in Alfred Habegger's

*My Wars Are Laid Away in Books: The Life of Emily Dickinson* (Random House, 2001), and her composition by fascicle (and engagement with George Herbert) in Sharon Cameron's *Choosing Not Choosing: Dickinson's Fascicles* (University of Chicago, 1992). The role of common meter and "Dr. Watts hymns" in the African-American religious tradition is treated in William Dargan's *Lining Out the Word* (University of California, 2006).

Louis Zukofsky outlines some of his method and sources for "A"–9 in the self-published pamphlet *First Half of "A"–9*, published in 1940 in a mimeographed edition of 55 copies. Further background on the poem appears in Mark Scroggins' *The Poem of a Life: A Biography of Louis Zukofsky* (Shoemaker & Hoard, 2007), as well as in the correspondence between Pound and Zukofsky collected in *Pound/Zukofsky* (Barry Ahearn, ed.; New Directions, 1987). Pound's translations of Cavalcanti, including his version of "Donna mi prega," are found in *Poems and Translations* (Library of America, 2003). The best study of Dante's friend in English is Maria Luisa Ardizzone's *Guido Cavalcanti: The Other Middle Ages* (University of Toronto, 2002), which also includes the correspondence between Pound and medieval historian Etienne Gilson.

Basil Bunting's "On the Fly-Leaf of Pound's Cantos" is collected in *The Poems of Basil Bunting* (Don Share, ed; Faber and Faber, 2016). The contemporary fashion of dismissing Pound on account of his (execrable) politics is facile and cuts poets off from the history of their art. Writers like Charles Olson and Robert Duncan considered the *Cantos* indispensable.

## on Rhyme

Pier Paolo Pasolini interviewed Pound, and Diane di Prima travelled to St. Elizabeth's to study with him. 'Nuff said.

When I was in Washington, DC, in 2014, just prior to giving the talk at Berl's, Rod Smith asked me: "Do you like Creeley?" I replied, "What do you mean?" He repeated, with some vehemence: *"Do you like Creeley?"* I said, "Yeah, I guess so?" Whereupon he gave me a copy of the then-brand-new *Selected Letters* (Rod Smith, Peter Baker, and Kaplan Harris, eds.; University of California, 2014), which I read on the bus, and from which I learned some about Creeley's interest in rhyme. Thanks, Rod.

These are the books I was thinking about, and thinking with, as I reflected on rhyme—its emergence, progress, inoperativity, and prospect. I hope there's something in here useful for you.

*David Brazil*
*New Orleans, Lent 2021*

The Yellow Papers 4: *A Talk on Rhyme* by David Brazil

*A Talk on Rhyme* is distilled from a talk given for the Leslie Flint Series at Berl's Poetry Store on October 17, 2014, as the first in a series of occasional presentations on fundamental issues in poetry. I wish to thank the proprietors of Berl's, Farrah Field and Jared White; Jamie Townsend, who invited me to present for the Leslie Flint series; Ian Dreiblatt, who introduced the talk; and Phil Baber, who commissioned this pamphlet. —D.B.

Published in 2021 by The Last Books, Amsterdam and Sofia
Printed and bound in the UK by Imprint

ISBN 978 94 91780 08 0

The Yellow Papers, edited and designed by Phil Baber, is a pamphlet series for poetics; see thelastbooks.org for back issues and subscriptions.

TYP 1: *The Following* by John Wilkinson
TYP 2: *The Politics of Delivery* by Holly Pester
TYP 3: *Blackfishing the IUD* by Caren Beilin